THINKER *vs* DOER

Tools to Get You Doing

JP Adams

© 2019 John-Paul Adams. All rights reserved.

Dedication

To the doers - thinking will tell you where.

To the thinkers – doing will get you there.

.

Contents

Dedication	3
Introduction	6
Part I	8
The Rodin Response	9
Thoughts: Exit Stage Left	19
The Self-Conscious Doer	23
Overthinking the Future	33
Part II	36
Discipline and Other Bad Words	37
Accountability and More Bad Words	49
Organized Thinking	58
Terms of Doing	69
Applications	78
Self-Testing for Doers	82
How to Do	86
Versus	91
Do it Like a Thinker	95

Part III	**99**
Real Problems vs First-World Problems	**100**
The Four Stages of Competence	**104**
Thinking About Doing Something	**109**
The Five Terms of Action	**115**
My Project	**119**
About the Author	**121**

Introduction

The majority of our adult desires are derived from our experiences as children. In this sense, most of what and how we think as adults is rooted in the thinking we did in the past. Ideas can therefore be defined as thoughts triggered by some familiar desire we have had buried in our minds. Ideas are much like seeds; once a seed has been planted, it will grow according to the level of nurturing it receives. What is important to understand is the type of nurturing the soil needs in order for that particular seed to grow its best.

As time has passed our desires have developed. There can be countless ways through which our desires grow, the issue becomes the typical obligations of adult life and how those obligations seem to have gotten in the way of our dreams, and what it is that we want from life. Time feels limited, money seems scarce, and relationships and family need consistency and attention. However, at some point we have to stop and consider the difference between surviving and living. Granted this might not be a particularly conscious realization at first, but you will nevertheless sense a dissonance between your thought-life and your doing-life. This book is for those of us who, having come to this realization, want more from life and rightly so!

What I hope for you to take from this book is confidence primarily; through understanding your conscious processes you will begin to understand and apply new ways of thinking and doing. At the core of my goal for this book, having been the person I've described, is to share the things I have learned to deploy – the things that have allowed me to succeed.

Take the time to clarify what your reasons are for picking up this book. Have you been hearing that call to make a shift? Do you, as I did, sense this profound disconnect between what you want your life to look like and what it actually looks like? I want to help you find the motivation and the discipline to discover your destination and work on your direction. That is what this guide is all about; your journey – a path that will lead you to satisfaction, and a joy you've probably not felt in a while.

Part I

The Rodin Response

Some people can go through their day without getting carried off in their thoughts and ideas. They can prioritize their tasks and complete their to-do lists without fail. If, like myself, you're more of a Thinker, such seemingly simple tasks may come with some difficulty.

Over the years you've had many ideas: ideas for projects, books, apps, businesses, services. Despite having these ideas and spending a considerable amount of time mulling them over in your mind, somewhere along the thought track you got off and hopped on another train. You have not launched any of these ideas, or perhaps not the ones you really wanted to. Rather than becoming destinations these ideas became stops along a wander. You took in the scenic views and, eventually, moved on.

The uncertainties of the results of action fill you with dread. So much so that you stop and focus on all of the possible pitfalls your actions may cause. This mode of thinking can work in your favor if what you do involves having to risk assess and minimize potential failures. The negative, and unfortunately frequent attachment to this kind of thinking however is stagnation, stemming from a fear of failure.

You may just be an idea-magnet. You're almost prolific when it comes to generating ideas. Again, this trait is not inherently negative.

However, if you have found yourself mid-way through a plan – substantial or not – and a new idea took over leaving you shifting from one thing to another, never completing anything, then your magnetism will only leave your ideas to rot in limbo.

This is The Rodin Response: to be stuck in a state of perpetual thinking and never doing. Our first goal then is to learn your natural inclination and how to use your individuality to your advantage, for your success.

The Graveyard

A graveyard is a simple thing; it is where we bury the dead. It is also the wealthiest place on the planet:

"There lie buried companies that were never started, inventions that were never made, bestselling books that were never written, and masterpieces that were never painted. In the cemetery is buried the greatest treasure of untapped potential."

- Dr. Myles Munroe

Whether you've killed them off or they've starved to death, you're left with a graveyard full of undead dreams. If there's one thing we've learned from horror movies, it's that the undead will haunt us until they're somehow laid to rest. Up until that point, these ideas will be floating around our minds. Perhaps you are aware of some of your ghosts; perhaps they're hiding in wait and keeping you up at night. Whatever their status is, you can be sure of one thing: they are taking up space – your focus is split – and you may not realize it.

You go from place to place in your mind picking up new stimuli and leaving behind old ideas. This is called drifting, and it is what causes ideas to become undead. Without clarity of destination, you'll go East when an idea calls from the North; you'll turn North, but another will call from the South. You keep turning, never stopping to figure out what it is you're searching for, never meeting your calls. Instead, you drift to the siren songs of the next new idea that claims to meet your needs, but if you chase two rabbits – so to speak – you'll catch none.

You will always find that one idea is calling you louder than the others. That one is yours. You have to stop drifting and learn how to navigate and set yourself a course to run, one that will guide you to your destination. Whatever struggles you find yourself in right now, know that there is and there has always been a calling on your life.

Thinking Ruins Everything

Within you there is both a Thinker and a Doer. Usually, one of them runs the show. The first step is to recognize which of these are dominant. It can be attributed to which sides of the brain are most active in a person, or which personality type they fall under. Thinkers will usually identify as introverts. This means that Thinkers will tend to see themselves as indecisive, shy, and going off in all directions at once unable to settle on a single career path or plan of any sort. Eventually, this belief will lead a person to feel that they are at fault somehow. They may have been told that they are procrastinators or plain lazy. I recently had a conversation about this with a friend, he told me thinking ruins everything. This statement stuck with me. I wondered how bad his experiences must have been to have driven him to believe this. I came to the conclusion that this sentiment exists as a result of inaction.

The sooner we realize that the problem of inaction isn't the Thinker's fault, the sooner we can activate the Doer. Thinking is a tool we use to solve problems and generate ideas. It is like a GPS system in that it will only serve you once you've punched in a destination.

Let us imagine then that you have set out on a road-trip with a good friend of yours. You've agreed to drive, and your friend will read the map and navigate the journey – planning the necessary stops and estimating your time of arrival. What if, through no bad intention, your friend decided to ignore the plan and make things up as you went along? If you were hungry, he'd direct you to a diner, even if that diner was off-route. If you were tired, he'd pick a motel at random, no matter if it was half an hour in the opposite direction. Maybe nature calls and your friend, knowing how much of a germafobe you are, takes you to the cleanest rest stop he knows. You get the idea. The plan is abandoned and you're driving from place to place satisfying your immediate needs, and never actually getting to where you need to be. Naturally you blame your friend, it was his job to navigate after all.

We start to think that the problems we have succeeding are due to thinking, but this was never the issue. The issue is and will always be that we cannot control our thoughts for they are products of imagination, experience, and desire, and they are infinite by nature. Our inner-Thinker can be a highly useful tool for success, but it needs a controlled environment to function productively. You are the one in control – you are the driver – and you decide where you want to go.

The mind is a system of transmitters and receivers, you are like a super, super computer. If you receive too much information at once, your *processor* will slow down and eventually crash. If you overfeed your mind it cannot be of use; there is a reason that GPS systems don't allow you to enter two destinations at once. Thinking doesn't ruin anything, you have simply let go of the wheel too long and have forgotten how to drive. It is important to remember that you are in charge, and while your mind will freely generate ideas, usually without your consent, you tell it what to focus on and what to discard.

Break Down to Build Up

Self-awareness is key to building or breaking a habit. Once you are aware of what you're doing or not doing, you can recognize if your habits are serving you well.

Over-thinking is a problem all on its own. Thinkers leave little space for themselves to consider how much time they put into thinking. We may not realize when and where our thoughts begin, or end for that matter. We will usually become aware of our thoughts after the fact. By this time, you may have lost several hours of the day. There are techniques to be learned that will help you to control your thought-train. The popular techniques out there are generalized, but since no two Thinkers are alike, no one technique will work for all Thinkers. This is why self-awareness is critical. If you can catch yourself at the beginning of the track, you can create a new habit of using your thinking to serve you better. You have to understand your natural tendencies and patterns to turn a passive activity into an active one that you can measure and direct. There are exercises that will help you discover how to understand your thought processes, and then what to do about it.

Get Out of Your Head

Free-writing, also termed stream of consciousness, is a style of writing in which thoughts and feelings are written in a continuous, uninterrupted flow. In other words, you do not prepare a thought before expressing it, you only express it. The term was coined in William James' Principles of Psychology (1890). This is the simplest, most effective way to track your thinking, and it has been around for more than a century. There are other effective ways to record your thoughts, though I highly recommend that you attempt free-writing, feel free to use the method with which you are most confident. You could use brainstorms, filming, voice memos, even annotated sketches. Having this control over the *how* can allow you to tune out the *what* until it's applicable.

As I've noted, free-writing won't come naturally to everyone. It is important to consider your wiring and your abilities. Ultimately, it won't matter which method you choose; whether you are unpracticed or unconfident. What is important is that you pick a method and try. You can always switch later.

Maybe your struggle is with the freely expressing yourself aspect. Perhaps you're not used to this or uncomfortable with it. The success of the activity depends on your commitment and the level of discipline you apply to the exercise. No one has to know that you're doing this, and no one has to see or hear what you record; it is all for your own benefit. If you need a push, I suggest conjuring up a question or a statement that relates to what you're struggling with. Write this at the top of your page or state it at the beginning of your recording, this is your starting point.

Whichever method you decide on, this activity can be daunting. Perhaps multiple attempts will be necessary before you are able to get into a flow. Remember, this is a conscious effort and an investment in yourself.

Free-Writing

I used this process to figure out why I wanted to write this very book, and what it was going to be about. Below I have included a section of that free-write, typos and all. I hope to illustrate the nature of the activity and the usefulness of it. A free-write does not have to be well-written, it must simply be an honest output of your mind. Like so:

"Who am I writing for? Right now I'm writing for people that are trying to figure out to go about making the book happen, and I think that people do not figure that out so I guess this is something that I will have to figure out here as well. I don't know who I'm writing for so now I have to stop and think about who is ti that I am trying to write for? More importantly, I have to make sure that I do not get myself cause up with the issue of trying to make sure that I'm right or that I'm solving the problems for me. Instead, I have to get myself out of the way and get to the place where I am focusing on helping other to figure out what they want. To that end, if I want this book to be a commercial success, then I might want to take a stab

instead and making an entirely different approach of finding every question that was asked on the redid channel and seeing that I can answer that. After all, the goal of this book is for it to be a commercial success and I think that this can do that. I know that even I think about that I have to figure out what it is that I have to do and this is like creating a documentary of what happens when some is taking an idea and bring it to life."

That is what you ought to expect from a free-write. The beginning of a free-writing session is initially useful for cutting through the noise in your head, to then allow you to reach a place of clarity. It may not make sense to anyone else, but it helps you think effectively. You'll be ready to explore what it is you actually want and how you can make that happen.

Countdown

Once you decide on a mode of expression, you must fix this activity to a timeframe in order to coax your thoughts from your mind – ready or not – and create a new thinking habit. It is best to start small: begin with five-minute sessions; then 10, then 15, and so on. Pick a thought that has been running your track for a while too long and see what spews out during this period. Planning time for this activity means setting aside a small portion of every day and letting nothing interfere with that. It typically takes a minimum of 21 days to form a habit, so give your brain the chance to recognize this new, consistent activity so that it may thereafter expect and support its continuation.

The Golden Nuggets

You will often find a lot of noise in your recordings: repetitiveness and straying are normal. Considering that your results depend entirely upon your commitment to the task, it does not matter how much time your thoughts spend on this loop. If you begin the task knowing there will be a scarcity of new and original thinking, you will help to pull your mind out of the usual idle worrying. You're mining for those golden nuggets of information, it should come as no surprise that these will be buried under mounds of redundant, repetitive thought.

Over time you will have built an awareness around how you think, catching yourself as you land on those indefinite worries and instead, build trust between where you are now and where you want to be. Recording your thoughts will help you to achieve a balance between thinking and doing.

Questions for Reflection:

- What are some treasures that are buried in your graveyard of unrealized dreams?

- Which ideas or plans are calling out to you?

- How have you gone off course and what methods can you use to bring your self back on track?

Thoughts: Exit Stage Left

How you go about getting your thoughts out of your head is nowhere near as important as doing it. Pick a thought that has been dominating your mind, choose a method that resonates with you, and do it.

Lists

This is a popular method of task ordering that provides structure to your daily dos. Many people will have tried to-do lists, not as many people will have actually benefitted from it. Though it remains a good and useful tool, it is one that has proven difficult to follow through with.

The purpose of a list is to capture that which has been sitting idly in your mind, to then enable you to attribute some order to your thoughts and ideas for the purpose of getting things done. Lists can be applied to various forms of action: outlining a plan for a project, storyboarding, or brainstorming. Most importantly, a list is a tangible thing. People tend to react differently when there is some physicality or reward involved. You see the items on your to-do list, and once you complete a task you earn the satisfaction of crossing that item out or drawing a little tick by it. This is called gratification. In its healthiest context, gratification is necessary for the progression of a desire to its given reward; it is the satisfaction received via the completion or achievement of one's goals and desires. This, of course, can be perverted – but we will cover that later.

Phone a Friend

Another idea-spewing activity is talking. This is somewhat underrated by the more introverted Thinkers. The assumption here is that you have friends or family with whom you are comfortable and secure. Understandably, if you have no such people this activity may prove to be difficult – but not impossible. There are always options, and if you are willing to try some of these options you may surprise yourself. You could start taking classes in a subject you enjoy and meet people that way; You could, if applicable, see a therapist or counsellor; You could strike up a conversation with a total stranger in a coffee shop. Regardless of how you find a friend, it will work in your favor to speak your thoughts to another person. We are social, relational creatures after all.

Having a conversation works, primarily because when someone is listening to you you won't get stuck on any single thought. This is because there will be input from a mind that is not your own. Countless times have I found myself stuck on a thought, looping around the same idea without concluding the matter. It takes trust and willingness to open-up your thinking to another person, but the minute you do you will broaden your perspective on the situation.

Feedback and critique are needed for improvement and effectivity. This principle can be likened to trial and error. Action will provoke results, and results will tell you how to proceed.

Talk to Yourself

It is totally sane and helpful to talk to yourself! Voicing your thoughts help to calm and clarify your mind. There is something to the act of verbalization that is cathartic. This activity creates what is called a bottleneck: speech naturally forces you to slow, sequence, and focus your thinking; you cannot speak and think at the same time. Open-up to yourself.

Wilson

If talking to yourself and talking to people is too weird for you, there are other places you can direct your speech.

The mind is a complex and sometimes silly place. Before I go on to reference this movie, I must call spoiler alert for those of you who have not yet seen it. In the film Cast Away, actor Tom Hanks plays FedEx courier Chuck Noland, enroute to Malaysia Chuck's plane crashes and he is stranded on an island with nothing and no one but a Wilson brand volleyball, upon which he draws a face and adequately names Wilson. He talks to Wilson, and the inanimate object listens to Chuck's thoughts, preventing him from insanity. Talking to an object means directing your speech at something, it seems ridiculous, but it is a genuinely helpful inbetweener.

Mind-Sweep

Mind sweeping is similar to free-writing, only structured. It is similar because your aim is to write down unfiltered thoughts. It is different because these thoughts will adhere to a bulleted structure. You list these for as long as is needed and by the end you will be able to examine what is occupying your mind. This benefits you by allowing you to identify everything that has your attention.

Questions for Reflection:

- What thoughts have you been ruminating on that you need to move out of your head?

- What approach resonates with you to get your unfiltered thoughts out of your head so you can examine them?

The Self-Conscious Doer

This can be a sore subject for some. There are as many valid reasons for a person to become self-conscious as there are areas effected by self-consciousness. It is a deeply sensitive issue that is almost always rooted in a fear of failure and its associate, embarrassment. I do believe it is imperative to understand our emotional and mental state, because without an understanding of our afflictions there can be no sufficient cure. However, I will refrain from making any such assumption of your personal afflictions and instead, offer you solutions relating to productivity and self-expression.

One of the struggles of being a Thinker relates to self-conscious behavior. Being in your head all of the time develops certain tendencies and effects how you see yourself. Usually when a Thinker imagines themselves doing something, their assessment of that situation is negative. It is far more difficult to picture yourself succeeding than to picture yourself failing, this is especially true of Thinkers that are not practiced Doers.

Let's shine a brighter light on this. The fact that you are able to vividly experience failure in your mind, means that it is possible to turn the tables on yourself and imagine instead, success. Keep in mind that when anyone tries anything that is new to them, they venture into the unknown; minor setbacks should be expected, but not taken as final.

Getting Caught Up in Self-Consciousness

Some may understand that feeling self-conscious at times is normal. An unpracticed Doer will struggle with setting this feeling into context and will become frustrated and stressed, believing there is something wrong with them. This sense of fear can be applied to the smallest of things, like answering a question in class or introducing yourself to a stranger. Being self-conscious can be a very simple thing to describe and put into perspective: you become aware of the potential risk associated to an action and are highly conscious of yourself in anticipation to this action. You focus on *how* you do the thing, rather than being focused on the thing you are doing.

It is important to note the term unpracticed Doer here, because there certainly are ways to break out of self-conscious behavior. You can reach a point within yourself where, though you may continue to feel jittery or nervous in some situations, these feelings will not stunt you.

144 Players

A study on the effectiveness of mentally practicing an activity or skill suggests that a person can imagine themselves to real improvement and success. The results of the study posed that the mentally practiced subjects reaped near the same results as the physically practiced. 144 basketball players were split into two groups; group A physically practiced one-handed free-throws, while group B only practiced them mentally. When each group was tested after two weeks, the players had improved by nearly the same amount.

Everyone knows that practice makes the master. That is why this is a useful study for Thinkers to consider. Try to practice something mentally, visualize yourself succeeding in a given situation in which you would usually feel self-conscious. Remember, this activity takes place in your mind first, there will be no real failure or embarrassment there. The purpose of this is to prepare you for the actuality of doing the thing you are preparing for - you cannot merely think-practice, the time for action must come. However, by consistently visualizing your success, your confidence will build. Whatever the situation is, practice will build the necessary skill and confidence.

Make it a Game

We often see this in parents with their children, making games out of chores. A game of your own creation means you can choose what it takes to win. Motivational public speaker and self-development author Brian Tracy told of a sales team that made a game out of rejection. The person who received 10 rejections by the end of the day would stand up and ring a celebratory bell, and their colleagues would applaud them. Naturally, no one likes rejection, but when that's the game you're playing your perspective changes, and there is no negative connotation attached.

This can be done in other ways, like a no-bad-idea brainstorm, or improv. There is an improv show called 'Whose Line is it Anyway?' The more ridiculous humor they attach to an otherwise embarrassing scenario, the better. The point is, whatever the game demands, you can exercise the power of intentionality to change what is perceived to be a win.

Know the Rules

Maybe creating the game isn't an option, perhaps there is already one in place. In this case, what are the rules of the game you're trying win? If you learn the rules, you can understand what it is about the game that makes you feel self-conscious. Through this understanding, you can use those rules to win.

When I decided to create a YouTube channel to share videos of myself speaking on particular subjects, it was nerve-wracking. I wasn't able to get my mind off whether or not I was being interesting enough, or whether the camera was at the best angle, or if anyone would even want to watch. I sat through these discomforts, unable to focus on anything other than the fact that I was being recorded. Eventually, I began to think about the rules of the game, and I realized what was making me so nervous. I was in a position where I could be talking to millions of people – strangers without faces. It's difficult to talk to a person you cannot see, it brings up an instinct of caution. I then discovered that I could bend this rule to my favor. I moved the camera slightly off center and started talking to my wife who was sat out of view. This simple alteration turned a daunting experience into one that I could familiarize with and become comfortable in.

Check Your Inventory

There is no better boost of confidence than to catch yourself doing something well. If we consider our primitive responses to experiencing danger and pain, it is understandable that we subsequently avoid scenarios where the same or similar threats are posed. This can also be ascertained through a psychological understanding; our unconscious mind will send signals via our nervous system to protect us from perceived danger based on negative past experiences. This provides an explanation of why we are physically afflicted by feelings of nervousness or stress. While both our primitive nature and our complex psyche have the good intention of self-protection, this does not always translate well in life. In fact, these signals will often stunt our growth and keep us from being self-confident adults.

If we train our brains to retain and reinforce positive experiences, we can begin to feel good about new opportunities and situations where action is necessary for success. We will only become self-conscious toward something that we believe we are no good at. This gap between self-belief and experience is what leads to self-consciousness and inaction, or ineffective action.

We ought to perform regular inventory checks. However small the success was, it's useful to remember the things you have achieved and are good at. The place in which you set your focus is the place that informs your perception. Keep memorabilia if possible, make a list of achievements and deeds; commit some successes to memory and actively recall those moments. Do these things so that when it's time for an inventory check, you will have a balance of your strengths and your areas to improve.

Being Self-Conscious and Doing it Anyway

To practice means to consistently perform an activity with the intent to improve. Practice pushing yourself out of your comfort zone, so that you may give yourself a chance to become used to the process of doing and become confident and secure.

What is the worst consequence of being a bad dancer at a party? People may laugh at you, making you feel stupid or inadequate. While that is an upsetting possibility, it is more important to consider a lifetime of never dancing in public because you are afraid of being judged. When you decide to dance, despite the potential heckling, you will realize that the only long-term consequence of doing something badly, consistently, is that you either lose nothing and stay bad at it, or you get better. Besides, people can surprise you. Perhaps instead of heckling you they'll support you, they may even admire you for stepping up and trying.

Self-consciousness is about control or the lack of. If you do decide to step up and do the thing that scares you, you will in that moment have taken control. You will either have the experience and decide it's not for you, or you'll want to improve at it. It is during the anticipation of an activity that gives your mind the space to control you; the longer you allow your mind to race through doubts and risks and fears, the harder it will be for you to take control and activate your inner Doer.

Find Your Reasons

Knowing why you want something can be the most powerful motivator for taking action. When you're dealing with something as flaky and fleeting as a desire, it is important to know why it is there and where you want it to take you. Finding the purpose in a desire is what sets us apart from other forms of life, the *why* is as important to us as the *what* and the *how*.

Kids Rule

Kids don't get hung up on failure; they are not self-conscious, they are bold and curious and persistent. Kids will boast of all the things they do well, they'll want to show you the cartwheel they haven't quite mastered yet, the all-over-the-place painting they've done, the crappy ceramic they made at school. They're proud of themselves, and it's great. Kids are Doer's, even the shy ones. They do still seek approval and need reassurance. The adults responsible for them ought to reinforce their self-belief. Unfortunately, it is often the case that as they enter into the world outside of themselves, negative influences creep in and cling on, challenging their self-esteem. Cases vary, but these influences can cause deep insecurities and fears. This is not to point the finger at the man, nor at the parents, necessarily. Opposition is simply a part of growth. I only wish to bring awareness to our original self-perspective in the hope of regaining it.

Focus on the things you do well and remember them. Look at your attributes and let yourself feel great and capable again. Imagine how it would feel to walk into a room full of strangers and own it; to attempt something without getting caught up in doubts; to be able to shrug your shoulders and smile after doing something badly, and just move on. Confident people simply have a can-do attitude, it may seem too cliché to be true, but clichés are clichés because they are so universally true.

You can put on confidence like a cloak. It isn't about genetics, upbringing, nor is it luck. It is an attitude you learn. Catch yourself doing something right, remember? Remind yourself of what you are capable of. Confidence is knowing you're capable.

I cannot stress the importance of being able to review your successes enough, I recommend carrying a notebook with you, always. If that's inconvenient, create a note on your phone or tablet. If you don't like to write or you have no time, use the default voice memo application on your smart phone, they've all got one. How ever you record your wins, you'll be building upon a more positive self-perception, one that will eventually become natural to you.

Recap

One of the struggles of being a Thinker relates to self-conscious behavior. Usually, when a Thinker imagines himself doing something, their assessment of that situation is negative. The fact that you can vividly experience failure in your mind, means that it is possible to turn the tables on yourself and imagine instead of success.

An unpracticed Doer will feel frustrated at being self-conscious: you are aware of the potential risk of action and are highly conscious of yourself in anticipation of this action. There are ways to break out of this self-conscious behavior.

Mental practice is one way to break out of self-conscious behavior. A study with two different groups of basketball players shows that mentally practicing a skill or activity can lead to real improvement and success. One group physically practiced free throws while the other group only mentally practiced. The players improved the same amount when later tested. Mental practice and visualization can lead to success in a situation where you would usually feel self-conscious.

Another tool to break out of self-conscious behavior is by making a game out of rejection or embarrassment. This can be done through a no-bad-idea brainstorm, or improvisation. By making a game out of denial, the negative connotation collapses by changing your perspective.

Simple alterations can also help. Understanding little specifics of what makes you self-conscious can help you work towards removing or altering those specifics. If talking to a big group of people you don't know is nerve-wracking, focus on talking to one person in the group you do.

If we train our brains to retain and reinforce positive experiences, we can begin to feel good about new opportunities and situations where the action is necessary for success. We ought to perform regular inventory checks. However small the victory was, it's useful to remember the things you have achieved and are good at. Keep memorabilia if possible, make a list of achievements and deeds; commit some successes to memory and actively recall those moments.

Practice pushing yourself out of your comfort zone, so that you may give yourself a chance to become used to the process of doing and become confident and secure.

You will realize that the only long-term consequence of doing something badly, consistently, is that you either stay bad at it, or you get better. Self-consciousness is about control or the lack of. If you do decide to step up and do the thing that scares you, you will at that moment have taken control.

Kids don't get hung up on failure or self-conscious. Adults can regain this. Focus on the things you do well and remind yourself of what you are capable of. I recommend carrying a notebook with you, always. If that's inconvenient, create a note on your phone or tablet or use the voice memo application on your smartphone.

Questions for Reflection:

- What is something specific that makes you self-conscious?

- What are three things that you know you do well?

- What is a skill you would like to improve through mental practice?

Overthinking the Future

Planning for the future is good if you plan to work towards your future plans – if you aren't planning on working towards your future plans, don't plan on it all working out.

We can desire many things, even contradictory things. Setting your eyes on something you want means more than thinking and talking about it. There may be things you desire but have no intention of trying for, we need to learn to discern between those things and the things we truly want to achieve. Otherwise, we become paralyzed by the sheer amount of desires we have.

Finish Your Thoughts

Finishing a thought or, in other words, putting it to rest is the best way to get your mind to let go of worrying about a goal you've set. You have to know the end as well as the means for your mind to let go.

Ask yourself this: what are you trying to solve? Think of your purpose as a solution to a problem. This will help lead you to and through structural thinking, so that you need not worry about your goals and plans every day. By stating the one thing that you are trying to solve, your thoughts of the future will become more productive and logical.

Prioritize and press pause on your future worries, allow yourself to focus on the present moment and deal with the tasks at hand.

A Someday Maybe List

The title of this exercise may seem counterproductive, it is in fact a helpful organizational tool. It begins in the form of a brainstorm, after which you sift through the ideas manifested and prioritize that which you wish to achieve sooner, and that which you wish to achieve *someday*. New interests and desires are inevitable but controllable. When you make a decision to work on something later and focus on something else now, you allow your mind to let those later goals go, until you decide to bring them forward.

If you're quite the organized old-fashioned sort, you can create this list in a journal or diary. However, if you want this to be as easy as possible, use an app. Create a folder for your goals to be reviewed periodically. The periodic reviewing is crucial to the success of this activity. The only risk of this exercise is to high idea-generating personalities. You may come up with a list too cumbersome to manage. In this case, you may find that grouping your lists is helpful.

Someday Maybe List Groups

Grouped lists are a more extensive way to contain your future plans and are best organized by areas of concern. Create a few categories, none of which should be for the miscellaneous. With this one rule, you eliminate idle worries.

Focus on discerning that which is useful to concern yourself with now, and file away the rest. Reducing your areas of concern will free you up. You will have decided on what is most important and fixed it to a timeline. One of my own categories is "Team". This frees me to address the immediate issues relating to my team while keeping record of the rather random ideas for their improvement. I am therefore able to afford the time to review and apply these less immediate concerns later, and eventually consolidate them into projects.

Questions for Reflection:

- What are some incomplete thoughts that you need to bring to a conclusion?

- What are some projects and plans that you need to push forward to be reviewed at a later date?

Part II

Discipline and Other Bad Words

There are certain unattractive words that cause a rebellion within us, as if there is something unnatural about them. In many of my conversations with others about getting things done, I have found myself avoiding particular words and phrases. I do this to avoid getting *too real* and causing tension or discomfort for the other person. I have to test the waters and tiptoe around certain subjects, it can be exhausting. Is this going to be a light, shallow interaction or will we be able to connect and speak honestly?

I have realized that, although we all may claim to want better quality lives, the amount of people who are actually willing to do something about it is slim. Most people seem content with just talking about their dreams of the future, some people are content with pretending they've got it all under control and simply want to look the part - you see the latter a lot on social media. There are those few people who really want to go for it. Whoever you are, in whatever circumstances you find yourself in, you ought to know that you are able to make the necessary changes and achieve your goals.

As we explore some of these bad words, I suggest that you pay attention to how they make you feel; are these words a common part of your vocabulary or do you steer clear of them?

These won't be dictionary definitions, these are concepts. You will notice that some words are synonymous of one another, but the connotations attached to them are different.

Discipline

Discipline is loaded for almost everyone, me included. If something implies discipline, it is as if my mind understands this to mean punishment. It truly is an unpleasant word, tied to the general image of a person bigger than you that forces you to do things you do not feel like doing. It feels restrictive, like it somehow opposes your freedom.

Self-discipline carries an even heavier weight, because there is no one forcing you to do the thing you ought to do, it's you. Why should we do something we don't want to do? You are free to do as you wish; you are free to decide against attaching discipline to a goal. However, the result of a lack of discipline is inaction, always, and without action nothing will change. Freedom then, in this context, would be the choice to implement discipline in order to achieve a goal. When we begin to see discipline as a trustworthy ally and not an enemy, we realize that with it, we are in control. If we let ourselves do whatever we feel like doing, ignoring what needs doing, we are captives of procrastination, of lethargy, and of apathy.

Result

Results tend to bring back memories of school. School seems to be the place where all that mattered were your results, and perhaps it was here that our disliking of the concept began.

When I would get my grades, I would be able to see how my efforts translated into reality; all of the studying, the homework, the time spent in class. The funny thing is, a kid who shows up to every other class half an hour late and sleeps throughout, gets results. A person who goes to the gym, but eats McDonalds after every workout, gets results. A result is nothing but the fruit of effort.

People will tend to make excuses for why they've failed. They'll tell themselves that something doesn't work for them because of this and that. The truth is you probably didn't put the work in. Unfortunately, there's no participatory award in life. Showing up is the first step, but there's a climb ahead.

Start by identifying what results you're after. Results needn't be so daunting, only realistic. We need results. We need specificity. If we do not recognize our losses, we won't know when we're winning.

Measurement

Measurement is an especially taboo word it seems. In a meeting I struggled to get my team to see that we were lacking the right metrics by which to measure our performance. I later realized that the struggle was due to the use of the word measure; people were uncomfortable with the idea of measuring their performance. If we do not tie our performance to a measurement, how can we know whether or not we are doing well? The metrics ought to be irrefutable; they ought to be numbers.

We have to become better at accepting the good in measurement. It is understandable to find this uncomfortable and deem it unfair. However, the real reason people tend to struggle with this concept is that accepting it means there will be no place to hide.

Pick a goal and tie it to a number. If you're trying to get fit and healthy, review your progress by measuring your body fat percentage, your body mass index, your weight; keep a food diary, count calories. If you want to be more productive, track your hours spent working and block off your leisure time. When you rid yourself of places to hide, you can account for and secure your shortcomings and your triumphs. I cannot claim this book will be a success, but I can say with certainty that I dedicated a minimum of 25-minutes to writing it every day. I am able to say that I put in the effort to reach my goal. That is the value in applying measurement to goals.

Goals

When you set a goal, it can feel as though you have set yourself up for failure. You risk breaking a commitment, one that you alone are responsible for keeping; no one is going to punish or judge you for quitting, you will only have yourself to answer to. This can hit your confidence just as hard as a public commitment. When you fail to meet a goal, no matter if you are able to justify it, you will feel disappointed.

This is why it is important to create short-term goals in sight of the long-term ones. You ought to be able to identify the steps it will take and the time you will need. The more understanding you have of this, the less likely you will fail or be discouraged. The challenge is putting in the effort. Form better habits and get rid of the detrimental ones; learn new concepts and educate yourself. Whatever the steps are for you, it will always take sacrifice. We would all like to believe that we deserve good things, this is why we set ourselves unrealistic goals. We want what we want, and we want it immediately. Goals have become a concept likened to New Year's resolutions – promises are made, yet hardly ever followed through.

You need to cut yourself some slack. You are capable; do not mistake this with being entitled. Goals are a matter of being capable of causing that which you wish to bring into effect.

Done

The way people interact with this word is interesting, to say the least. When you apply a finite term to something, you'll be surprised by how desperately people dance around it.

You would think a person would be relieved at the completion of something, so that they can celebrate and acknowledge a win. Instead, you'll see people avoid the responsibility of completion. I have found that this sense of the word comes from perfectionism. The reason one might want to avoid claiming something is finished, is because they worry that it is not perfect, and they do not want that fact to reflect their own fallible nature. It is quite a beautifully human sentiment, though it is not at all helpful.

Deadline

A deadline is like a race, you must run the race in order to finish, and running takes commitment. When there is the set boundary of a deadline within which you must work, you have more clarity towards your potential failure, or success. It creates pressure.

When it comes to personal deadlines, you ought to deal with yourself with grace. Perhaps you complete your given task a day late, it may not matter. That however, is a dangerous game to play with yourself; "I'll just get it done when I can." you might say. What you are actually saying is that your goal doesn't matter enough, and there are more important things that deserve your attention. If that is true, you ought to check your inventory. Personally, I'd hate to leave something open-ended. Having a time constraint allows you to contain your efforts. In a way, you are more able to predict a win.

I might want to lose 20lbs, and if I wait long enough, I'll lose it effortlessly, as I deteriorate in my grave. I hope you understand the sarcasm there. Boundaries matter.

Purpose

This requires some upfront thinking, you need to be clear and honest about the reasons you want what you do – you can be sure that these reasons won't always be good, nor necessarily in your best interest. We must learn to discern between desires.

When I was getting clear on my reasons for writing this book, I found that one was to prove to people that I could do it. I didn't like this because it suggested I'm not as confident as I believe and as I have led others to believe. The fact remains, this was one of my reasons. The reason this was important for me to identify is because there is a part of me that says, "If I was capable, I would have done it by now, and it wouldn't be this hard.". It may be difficult for me to admit having this self-doubt, but it was imperative to acknowledge that voice because only then could I choose to ignore it, and instead, stick to the commitment I had made.

People will avoid self-reflection for one of two reasons: either, they prefer to deal with themselves on a solely surface level, or they refuse to face their reasons because they would rather not deal with the roots of their desires. While we may not like what our reasons say about us, it is only by acknowledging them that we can find the motivation to become the people we would proudly admit to being.

Ambition

Ambition is one of the more acceptable words of the bunch. Everyone likes to call themselves ambitious, it's something we've all had written on our resumes. There are some people however, who aren't as open about their ambitions. It is sometimes due to a highly self-critical way of thinking. To these people, being ambitious is equivalent to being greedy, and it means we are ungrateful, wanting of too much.

There are points where ambition can begin to yield returns that are more bad than good, that's greed. Ambitions are simply the aspirations of growth, and we ought to aspire to better.

Clarity

The reason we avoid being clear and specific about our needs is similar to why we dislike results. Without clarity, we can interpret away the reasons we did not succeed, wavering responsibility.

Having a clear understanding of what you want is essential. You should be able to see it and communicate it. Leave nothing to abstractions and interpretations, consistently remind yourself of what it is through documented examples. Being unclear of your goals is like leaving your backdoor unlocked and announcing it to your enemies. I mean to say that going forward with an idea without clarity leaves you vulnerable to influences that will throw you off track.

Productivity

One definition of productivity that has stuck with me is: when you are moving towards your goal or pre-defined objective, then you are being productive. I like this definition, it is simple, clear, and accurate.

Many people will equate productivity to time spent working. That, as mentioned, is measurement; it is a tool. There can be lots of activity, but if your activities are ineffective and do not lead you towards something specific, it is not productivity.

Earl Nightingale defines success as "The progressive realization of a worthy ideal.". That sounds a lot like productivity to me. Close the door in the face of excuses and misinterpretations. Modify your conceptualizations of these words, and simply allow them to serve you.

Focus

Focus is keeping your eyes on the prize, which is easier said than done for the high idea-generating people. I for one find it difficult. If we could figure a person's focus according to tasks, it would translate best as a percentage. If your mind is focused on one task, it has 100% of your attention; on two, it drops to 50%; three, 33%: four, 25%. The more things you focus on at one time, the less efficient each thing will become. The common standards for grading exams in schools are to help students achieve their best result by defining the percentage goal that constitutes a pass or fail. E.g. scoring below 60% is a fail where I went to school, our aim then was to score above that mark.

Not all tasks will require 100% of your focus, but your odds of success rise in relation to your level of concentration. If you try to do too many things at once for a prolonged period of time you will surely burn out, and at that time you will look back over your work and realize your results lean on quantity over quality. For this reason, delegation, time-management, and prioritization are key tools that we should practice and apply daily. To do this, you will have to be able to hone your efforts on one thing for a set amount of time. It is best to start with small numbers, you could start by dedicating a full five minutes to free-writing per day, or any other relevant task.

These days we seem to suffer from a disorder known as FOMO: fear of missing out. Quite the copout, would you agree? The fact is, focus requires us to refuse some things for the sake of other things. In its most productive form, focus will mean doing the thing you need to do now, in order to secure yourself in whatever proclivity later. Don't step over dollars to pick up dimes - invest in yourself.

Recap

Most people see discipline as implying punishment and restriction. However, the result of a lack of discipline is inaction, always, and without action, nothing will change. When we begin to see discipline as an ally and not an enemy, we realize that with it, we are in control.

As such, you should identify what results you're after. Make them realistic and specific. To see results, you have to put the work in and measure it.

For example, if you're trying to get fit and healthy, review your progress by measuring your body fat percentage, your body mass index, your weight; keep a food diary, count calories. If you want to be more productive, track your hours spent working and block off your leisure time.

Set short-term and long-term goals. You ought to be able to identify the steps it will take, and the time you will need. The challenge is putting in the effort. Form better habits and get rid of the detrimental ones.

Boundaries matter. Define the limits of what you are setting out to accomplish and by when.

Be clear and honest about the reasons you want what you want. We must learn to discern between desires. Acknowledging self-doubt is imperative.

Be ambitious and have a clear understanding of what you want is essential. You should be able to see it and communicate it.

And remember that you're only productive when you are moving towards your goal. Time spent does not equal productivity.

As long as you keep your eyes on the prize, your odds of success will rise with your level of concentration. And don't forget that time management and prioritization are vital tools that we should apply daily. To do this, you will have to be able to hone your efforts on one thing for a set amount of time.

Questions for Reflection:

- What results are you after?

- What are some short-term goals you can identify?

- How can you tie your goal/result to a number?

- What are the reasons you want what you want?

Accountability and More Bad Words

By now you will have noticed the codependency among these concepts. You may also have realized that you've heard many of them before, perhaps too many times to take them seriously and not disregard them as tricky marketing tools or clichés. You wouldn't be wrong, but you'd be missing the point.

We associate this vocabulary with motivational speakers. They love these words as much as you and I may hate them. Cliché or not, we listen to their talks and we buy their books because we want something they have. There is nothing wrong with admitting this to be true, you ought to – it's okay to want success, and it's even better to want to know how to get it.

Accountability

To be accountable is to be on the frontlines of your own war. The success of a goal depends on the sturdiness of its foundation and the integrity behind your commitments to it. If your goal is to do x and instead you do y, taking responsibility for that decision and accepting its consequences is accountability.

The reason this is an integral part of success is that it is partnered with your motivations, and we all need motivation. Find a partner whom you trust to be honest with you, I would suggest reaching out to someone with whom you share a professional relationship with, rather than personal. Agree on a schedule of checking-in with each other to keep you both on track.

Delayed Gratification

A study was done on the effects of delayed gratification with children. Each child was left alone in a room with one marshmallow. They were told that if they didn't eat that marshmallow right away, they would have two later. Unsurprisingly, some kids waited, and some didn't – adorable. What is most exciting is that these kids were followed up years later, and the results of the children, now adults, who were able to wait back then, were generally more successful later.

The principle is the same with money. People struggle with saving money because it is difficult to resist spending it. Saving your money will benefit you later, which is a reward you cannot experience right away. Buying yourself a new pair of shoes on payday however, feels great immediately. If we apply the discipline now, and skip the indulgent slack-time, our rewards will be bigger, better, and more useful later.

Meditation

Also referred to as mindfulness, there are immediate religious or spiritual associations with this concept. However, if we take the word at its root, and apply it in a literal sense, we find no necessary attachment to such things. Every word has an origin, the meanings of words are adopted and adapted to different agendas. Meditation means to reflect, study, and practice. It is a period of time you secure in which you will focus on something intensely. Practicing meditation can help train your mind to filter thoughts of the past and future, allowing you to focus on present matters.

If we let go of the typical connotations of this word, we will find in it a useful tool to help us along our journey from Thinker to Doer.

Commitment

Commitments follow decisions. To commit is to follow through on a decision, or vow; a concept that is lost on many. Commitment has become the pick and choose sort, we seem to have forgotten the necessity of it and with that, the power in it.

When it comes to getting results, there is nothing stronger than a sheer willingness to hold firmly to the decision of getting results. As a tool, it is relatively personal and therefore varied as to how you determine something to be worth your while, but it always takes investment, and an internalization of the idea that you will stand for something.

Public Commitments

Committing publicly to an action brings about a sense of accountability, ideally unattached to fear of punishment, rather attached to an ambition to succeed, with witnesses. Perhaps that seems superficial to some, but for the purposes of achieving a goal I believe it is highly effective, considering the relational nature of human beings. Feeling responsible for your success is a driving force that not everybody can jumpstart alone. If a person outside of yourself can hold you to your word, there's a helpful pressure to move forward.

This may cause too much pressure for some Thinkers, in which case I believe you may have told the wrong person. Personally, I needed to announce my goal of becoming a published author to as many people as I could. I sent posts out on Facebook and Instagram. Friends, family, co-workers, they all knew. This, for me, was an action toward securing my progress. There was no way I would back out – I had no place to hide.

Personal Commitments

A personal commitment is between you, and you. You are the only person who knows that you have committed to something; a promise to yourself to follow through on something that matters is a powerful and admirable trait. You could have it written out like a contract, or it could be a simple verbal agreement, whichever holds you more accountable.

Work

Work is the reason we hate Mondays. It really isn't Monday's fault, honest. Experience has shown me that it isn't work we hate, it's the thing we apply it to. Work will always be tied to laboriousness and toil, but we all do it. Why?

I recently took the time to meditate on what work means to me, I suggest you do the same. Why do I work? Up until a few years ago I worked for the sake of providing for my family, I hadn't ever considered a reason beyond that, perhaps because I wasn't aware that I needed one. As I mulled this concept over in my mind, a revelation hit. We all have dreams for the future, we all have images of what we want from life; work is the process of these intangibles becoming tangible.

There are legitimate reasons besides this to work, those are predominantly tied to money. While that is an unfortunate necessity of life, we ought to embrace work in its true purpose, in whatever capacity we can.

Early

The early bird does indeed catch the worm. Early means being the first person at a meeting or waking up early to get a head-start on your to-dos. Being early is one of the first signs of success.

Show up before everyone else, people respect you for it because it shows a level of commitment and seriousness. If something matters to you or if you have made a decision to be somewhere, see someone, or do something, make the effort to arrive early and show off your willingness and dedication.

Late

This doesn't mean having a lie-in on a Saturday morning, this means working late; putting in the hours to complete a project and achieve something. It's important to stick to timeframes, especially when it comes to your goals, but don't be afraid to spend a little longer on something worthwhile.

Challenge

This is one of the more neutral concepts, it is what you make of it. Being challenged by a thought or an action outside of our comfort zone can be difficult to want to accept. Why should we? We should because when something challenges you it is an opportunity to learn and to grow. By expanding your comfort zone, you become more resilient professionally and personally. A challenge now will later be described as an experience, the difficulty will pass, and you'll be left with new information about yourself.

However, if you instead fight and become defensive of challenges, you are refusing growth and will therefore stunt your progress. We were built for much more than comfort.

No

No is one of the most difficult words to use. It isn't always that we don't want to say no, it's that we don't want to *have to* say no. Saying no requires the same strength as self-discipline and serves us similarly by setting and maintaining boundaries.

You have to be able to say no to the things that distract or interrupt your commitments. This doesn't mean being a workaholic, it means prioritizing your needs and activities.

Standards

Imagine a co-worker is up for the same promotion as you. You are both punctual, educated, and capable of taking on further responsibility – for all intents and purposes, the playing field is level. How will your boss decide? You guessed it, standards.

Identify the bare minimum standard of a given goal, this will inform you of what can be taken further and how. Your standards will determine the quality of performance you are willing to provide and receive. The people whom you regard as high performers are simply people with high standards to which they consistently work.

Recap

Taking responsibility for a decision and accepting its consequences is accountability. The reason this is an integral part of success is that it is a partner with your motivations. Find a partner whom you trust, to be honest with you. Agree on a schedule of checking-in with each other to keep you both on track.

If we apply the discipline now, our rewards will be bigger, better, and more useful later.

Take time to reflect, study, and practice. It is a period you secure in which you will focus on something intensely in the present.

Follow through on your decision and vows. When it comes to getting results, there is nothing stronger than a sheer willingness to hold firmly to the choice of getting results.

And if you do this publicly, it will bring about a sense of accountability. If a person outside of yourself can hold you to your word, there's a significant pressure to move forward.

A promise to yourself to follow through on something that matters is just as important and admirable trait.

Do the work to make the intangibles you want to become tangible. Money is a necessity of life and we ought to embrace the real purpose of work when we can.

Be first as it is a sign of success. It shows a level of commitment, seriousness, and dedication. Then put in the hours to complete a project and achieve something, handling the challenges as they come.

Say no to some things. Saying no requires the same strength as self-discipline and similarly sets up and maintains boundaries. You have to be able to say no to things that distract or interrupt your commitments to prioritize.

Identify the bare minimum standard of a given goal; this will inform you of what you can take further and how. Your rules will determine the quality of performance you are willing to provide and receive.

Questions for Reflection:

- What are some standards you can hold yourself to?

- What is a public commitment you can make?

Organized Thinking

The typical reason behind active thinking is to process information and discover answers or possibilities. This isn't necessarily something we do intentionally, these are normal activities. Once you add intention to your thoughts, you're giving them a goal. Depending on your goal then, your thoughts will begin working towards a conclusion, rather than remaining haphazardly scattered.

If you are trying to clarify and understand something, you should consider applying the Feynman technique. That is, to explain the thing to yourself as if you were explaining it to a five-year-old child. This allows you to break the thing down into sizeable chunks.

We ask ourselves questions to figure out how to solve problems. In order to find solutions, we need to identify the causes and consequences. When your thoughts begin to overcome your ability to move forward, you need to stop and switch to doing something unrelated like tidying, going for a walk, the dishes; something physical is best. The reason your thoughts take the reins and become confused and stunted, is because you are asking yourself a series of questions that are either irrelevant, inaccurate, or nonsensical. Clarify your questions to organize your thoughts, otherwise you will be like a car stuck in a ditch - putting the pedal to the metal, burning rubber and exhausting fuel, yet going nowhere.

Idle Thinking

Your mind works even in the absence of consciousness, it doesn't need our input. We however, need its output. We must therefore be active Thinkers. Recall the last time you were seriously thinking about something trivial; I once spent three hours debating myself on whether I should go to the gym for 45 minutes or write for 25. How ridiculous is that! I wasted three hours trying to decide to do either of two activities which, together, would only have taken me 1 hour and 5 minutes.

Letting your mind run amok is not thinking, just as having a child is not parenting. Idleness is a time-wasting activity that requires zero conscious effort. Creative Thinkers tend to fall into idle behaviors. These people will come up with great ideas and perhaps even inspire others, but ultimately reaping no good for themselves. Letting your mind jump from one thing to another is not effective, it is indecisive.

To be clear, idle thinking does have its place. Letting your mind drive you from place-to-place can help stimulate creativity and aid problem-solving activities. Its place is essentially within brainstorming.

Productive Thinking

The only form of productive thought is thinking tied to an objective. This objective will be whatever it is you desire the result of your work to be – result being the key word here.

There aren't a lot of must-dos in this book, but result is one of the most necessary components of success. Get yourself a goal. The moment you apply your thinking to an understanding of a desired result, will be the moment you go from idle to productive.

Doing Without Thinking

An action without purpose is the same as a thought without an objective; it will move you, but not in any particular direction. This is something to keep in mind.

Doers are not more productive simply because they're impulsive or action-oriented. You can busy yourself for 12 hours straight, it won't necessarily mean you have been productive. Doers are no better than Thinkers, we both need to learn to move in a more measured and purposeful manner.

Productive Doing

Ideally, we want to be organized Thinkers and productive Doers. Productivity is result driven. Without a clear idea of what you want, your thoughts and actions will not have led you anywhere purposeful.

For the production of this book I wrote between 1,500 to 1,800 words per day for 28 days. That was according to my approximate typing and thinking speed. At this pace, I was able to achieve my goal of writing a 50,000-word draft in a month.

If my goal was to then publish this book in 45 days from the time I began writing, I would know that I needed to write for an hour per day in order to delegate focused time later, to research publishing, marketing, and editing.

This extensive measuring and planning required sacrifice. I have a wife, a toddler, and a job – important areas of my life that need my attention. When I am home, I find that I have a limited and sometimes unpredictable amount of time to myself. We all have to account for our personal time. For me to finish this book, I had to make sure I dedicated some or all of that personal time to writing.

There were a few days I felt too tired to write, and I once chose to redirect that designated writing time to Googling: pros and cons of hiring an editor. Was that productive? It could have been if I had already decided on whether to hire an editor or not. If that decision had been made, it would have been a good use of time because it would have been directed thinking. I would also have been able to properly account for the time needed to explore the idea. I should have maintained my focus on my writing goal, and not allow other thoughts or feelings to cut into what was already a limited time.

When you are doing things that lead you to the outcome that you're focused on, you're being productive. Otherwise, you're procrastinating. Some days I spent more time on my social media than I did on writing.

Though this is related to my goal, it wasn't what needed my immediate attention. The reality is that I wanted to avoid having to write because I didn't feel like it.

When you understand productivity in this way, you are able to properly prioritize and make progress. I must add that I am not advocating some insane level of rigidity, I am advocating sacrifice for the purpose of a better quality of life. For example: at the cost of missing one episode of my favorite show every night for a month, I was able to produce a book. I achieved something I had wanted to achieve for years in the short period of one month. It wasn't a matter of depriving myself of fun activities, it was a matter of not spending my designated writing time watching television.

There were other days I was so tired I would nod off, but I had still showed up to that appointment with myself to write, even if it was for 10 minutes. I was certainly productive, and I know this because I made progress.

Going from Thinking to Doing

We all do this, it's easy. I can go from contemplating all that I am grateful for in my life to watching Housewives of Atlanta; I could think up ideas on how to develop my business then scroll through Facebook for an hour.

What we're looking for however, is the kind of switch that takes a purposeful thought to a productive do. This means breaking the habit of idle daydreaming and aimless action and creating the habit of focus and productivity. It's neither smooth nor easy; it's a mission.

After we clarify our desired result, we can identify the space to get moving toward it. You can begin to understand your priorities, step-by-step. All the while able to keep calm and sure of yourself and your destination. Be protective of the free time you have and use it efficiently.

If we make this a practice, being productive will become second-nature. Once this balance of productive thinking and doing is embedded in your behavior and activities, you will be the kind of person that gets the right results.

Time in Context

Among the long list of things we avoid doing because we believe it will take too long – some trivial, some significant – living purposeful, rewarding lives is at number one.

We often fail to realize the context of time spent. We tend to prefer short-term gratifications far too much. If there's nothing of particular importance to you right now, try to recall a time when you put something important off because you figured it would take too long.

Put this thing into context by comparing it to the other things you did or do instead. I can spend many idle hours debating whether or not to work-out, I do not immediately realize the actual time-wasting I'm doing. We aren't all that natural at measuring time, I believe this is because time isn't a tangible experience, it is a transcendent implication of life - whether we like it or not.

Binge watch your favorite show on Netflix and you'll see how time flies, but turn your attention to work and you'll feel like you've aged five years in five minutes. The problem we all face is experiencing time like an emotion, it is something that again, is rooted in a fear of failure. If we are afraid of a potential result, not only will we influence a negative outcome, but every second leading up to that visualization will be agony. That is, until we decide to step-up and face the issue.

Time is our truest currency, it ought to be used as an investment and spent wisely. Within every restraint or boundary are options and possibilities; our human anatomy bounds us to the land, but we envied the flight of birds, so we built airplanes instead.

Context is the circumstance surrounding a thing. In this casing of time our experiences are shaped according to if and how we understand this context. This determines how we enter into any given moment. In other words, our experience of time is subject to the notion of inertia; the desire to remain in a particular state or experience. Inertia is quite a natural tendency of ours. If you're enjoying a run through the park, you wouldn't want to abruptly stop and go sit on the couch. Likewise, the same person could be lazing on the couch, feeling a resistance to getting up and going for a run.

The transition from one state to another feels like an interruption, regardless of whether the state is good or bad.

The Snooze Button Effect

One of the biggest mistakes we can make while attempting to be more successful is hitting the snooze button. It is difficult enough finding the will to get up early and do the thing you said you were going to do, without having to make the treacherous decision of whether to hit the snooze button or not.

A bloody battle ensues within your entire being when the decision comes for you to either leave your bed and go for that morning run or tell yourself the most common lie known to man: "five more minutes". You close your eyes, truly believing the lie, only to open them once more to find an hour has past. Getting up at your first alarm feels like a hellish ordeal, there seems to be no satisfactory reason to sacrifice those cloud-like pillows of comfort for such torture – unless you are a masochist.

In its immediate context, those extra five minutes seem like an insignificant amount of time. In its proper context, the circumstances surrounding that decision could be spending the final 30 years of your life with joint pains, weak muscles, perhaps something worse. Trading those five extra minutes for your long-term health is a pretty sweet trade, right?

Your momentary decisions inform the rest of your timeline. Once we have acclimated to a healthier, more intentional habit swap, our in-the-moment decisions will begin to create a better experience of time.

Five More Minutes

Your experience of time will change from the way you feel in anticipation - or at the beginning of - every new activity, to how you will feel once you have put that activity into practice. The day you decide to leave your bed, put on your running gear and get out the door – even if you start with a short walk – will be the day you begin an entirely different experience.

By putting the time it takes to do something into its proper context, we can see time as it is instead of how we feel it is. This shift means looking through the lens of your initial motivations, so that when the time comes for action you are not talking yourself out of it because you think it will take too long or you'd rather do something more immediately rewarding.

By contextualizing your time, you are continuously putting yourself back in touch with your purpose; the *why* that led you to want to make a change in the first place.

How to Put Time into Context

Specificity is the key to nailing this habit. Think of the action you want to take and create a realistic timeline. If you want to learn an instrument, how much time needs to be put into daily practice; what is the least amount of time you must spend on practicing? Get clear on the numbers, and your reasons: Why do I want this? What am I resisting?

After you've cleared it with yourself, get moving. These steps will help to increase your motivation, and they will make action easier the more you practice them. Go ahead and start something, even if it's the next chapter.

Recap

The common reason for thinking is to process information and discover answers or possibilities. If you are trying to clarify and understand something, you should consider applying the Feynman technique. That is, to explain the thing to yourself as if you were explaining it to a five-year-old child.

When your thoughts begin to overcome your ability to move forward, you need to stop and switch to doing something unrelated. We must be active Thinkers. Letting your mind jump from one thing to another is not practical, it is indecisive. Idle thinking can have its place — for brainstorming.

The only form of productive thought is thinking tied to an objective. Get yourself a goal. Doing without thinking is not productive either. An action without purpose is the same as a thought without a target. Both Doers and Thinkers need to learn to move more purposefully.

Productivity is result driven. Without a clear idea of what you want, your thoughts and actions will not have led you anywhere purposeful. When you are doing things that lead you to the outcome that you're focused on, you're productive. Otherwise, you're procrastinating.

When you understand productivity in this way, you are able to prioritize and make progress properly.

What we're looking for is the kind of switch that takes a purposeful thought to productive action. We tend to prefer short-term gratifications far too much. Time is our most dependable currency; it ought to be used as an investment and spent wisely. Your quick decisions inform the rest of your timeline. By putting the time it takes to do something into its proper context, we can see time as it is instead of how we feel it is.

Think of the action you want to take and create a realistic timeline. Get clear on the numbers, and your reasons: Why do I want this? What am I resisting? Then, get moving.

Questions for Reflection:

- Do you have a clear idea of what it is you want?

- What is a realistic timeline for what you want?

Terms of Doing

Familiarize yourself with the terms populating the productivity space. This will help your perspective and your confidence. My hope for this book is for it to be your starting point on a journey to a happier, more successful life. Understanding the language of success is a crucial part of that mission. After this chapter, you will be able to survive productive situations – whether it's reading an article or attending a networking event – without having to Google words and phrases. You'll be in the loop!

Life Hacks

This is a popular term that essentially describes shortcuts. A life hack is a way of doing things that is more time-efficient, and therefore better. In other words, it is a strategy, technique, or tool.

This becomes relevant to your journey once you have decided to be better at doing and have specified your goal. Otherwise, there is a common trap in which people tend to fall. That is, they binge watch irrelevant lifehack videos, never actually using the techniques either because these will have nothing to do with the person's goals, or the person is unclear on their goals, and are simply procrastinating.

By all means, hack away. So long as you have identified your motives and goals, it is a good strategy to apply. The more you understand the usual methods of doing a thing, the better able you will be at implementing time-efficiency to that thing. Set a time for experimentation.

Agile Results

The word to focus on here is agile. There are many books related to business that explore this concept. There is a specific book called *Getting Results the Agile Way* by J.D. Meier.

In computer programing there is no room for ambiguity. The programmer must write the software precisely according to how it ought to run, and what it ought to do. It is just as difficult for an individual to instruct themselves or instruct others to get things done. The formula for this is crucial, and we can apply it to our usual lives. The book prescribes much structure and formatting, as you might expect from a computer programmer. However, the most important aspect is the plan. For every task that you plan to do, you need be clear on a title for your outcome, the reasons you are doing it, how you plan to achieve it, and a definition of done.

As it relates to Thinkers and Doers, an agile result is the complete framework of how to deal with your tasks and goals, both short and long term.

TEA

TEA has been predominantly popularized by the company, Asian Efficiency, though it isn't a particularly new idea. The acronym stands for time, energy, and attention. The idea is that you cannot manage time by itself; you must be aware how you spend your energy and what has your attention.

This is a good concept to internalize, as I'm sure you would agree that it is not always a lack of time that prevents us from excelling. If you are exhausted or focused on something else, having time on your hands won't necessarily help you to tackle something that requires a certain mental sharpness. I have internalized this concept in its acronymic form, but also as a literal association; I have created an association with drinking green tea while I write, which has acted as an internal signal to work. I will sip my green tea and naturally be prompted for go time. This may not do anything for you, it is only an example of how you might implement a productive concept – by building an association with it that will prompt you.

GTD

GTD simply stands for getting things done. This is a term coined by David Allan. He came up with a method to help his clients get things done. His book was a big deal when it came out, and it continues to inform much of what and how we do in terms of the productive space.

The crux of GTD was that you should not keep anything in your head. Instead, you ought to capture it and organize it in the most appropriate list. This is so that when the time comes, and you are in a place where you can work it out, you can simply pull it up and begin.

RPM

The rapid planning method was created by Tony Robbins. RPM is significantly different from all the other concepts, because it focuses on outcomes and blocking. Blocking is a visual aid to help you organize your outcomes.

Simplified, RPM encourages us to look at our outcomes; our purpose for going after them, and the actions needed to get us closer. This helps us to avoid taking random actions towards unclear outcomes, which is an unproductive use of our TEA.

RPM spawned from the OPA (outcome, purpose, action) planner. This was created in the late 80s.

Kanban

Another visual based aid to arrange your tasks. Kanban involves using a physical space to create three columns: To-Do, Doing, and Done. You then add post-it notes with tasks written on them and place them in the relevant columns. As simple as it sounds, it's highly effective because of its visual and physical aspects. Kanban is the other giant in the room, next to GTD, as far as its influence on the way productivity apps are designed.

Kanban is based on something called a value stream. A value stream is like the steps of a staircase. For example, if you are writing a book, the value stream is the idea, topic, outline, draft, edit, done. The titles of each column can be specified to the task you wish to complete. One necessary filter however, regardless of the task, is to limit the amount of work per column. In the instance of writing a book, you could limit your draft column to two, and your edit column to one. This ensures a smooth work flow and avoids you becoming over-encumbered.

Spreadsheets

Believe it or not, people still use Microsoft Excel. As far as productivity tracking goes, it's quite the versatile tool. In fact, I would go as far as to say all of the newer, more interactive, appealing software available today was derived from the simple natured, outdated programs like Excel. You can collect all your tasks, add a column for tracking different stages and get a lot of utility out of google sheets or any other spreadsheet app out there.

The fancier tools out there can be more of a distraction than a simple logging tool. While spreadsheets are one of the most efficient ways to inspire and track progress, I would suggest using spreadsheets for larger projects.

The 12-Week Year

The idea is to take the things you wish to achieve in a year and plan it over a 12-week period. This is to improve your chances of getting on and actually executing your goals. I must admit, I have tried this method a few times, but I didn't get far. However, the reason I'm advocating it is to make a point; not all methods will suit all people. You may prosper with this activity, and I have heard enough good about this tactic from others to know that it just wasn't for me, but it may be for you.

Bullet Journal

You will find many paper-based planners, calendars, and diaries, the bullet journal is something quite different. The design is relatively simple and can be implemented in any notebook. There is nothing to buy, only a concept to apply.

Keeping a bullet journal is a brilliantly flexible progress tracker. You can fit it to whatever project you have going on, even customize it to the way you prefer to work. Having a system based on a pen-to-paper activity is really quite handy, it limits the surrounding distraction of upgrades and add-ons, and it will encourage honest entries.

The only downsides would be space and convenience. With digital applications you have an incredible amount of save space; a page in a notebook can only fit so much. However, I have found that the restrictions I impose on my digital tools would come naturally to an analogue method.

A bullet journal remains an excellent approach to structure and organization. There is little rigidity and it's definitely more adaptable and personable.

Auto-Focus

Auto-Focus is another pen-to-paper productivity system. It's a specific algorithm you use to process a list of things to do, set up to allow you to overcome the resistance toward getting started and doing.

You will find more than one version of it as the creator is always tinkering with the systems based on feedback from users. It isn't a particularly well-known method, but it is one of the more effective ones. There aren't many applications that model it, nor are there many books that take from it. Regardless of its obscurity, on the days I feel overwhelmed by tasks, this is my go-to system. Auto-focus is one of the most effective and easily implemented systems available; it's useful with minimal tech requirements.

Auto-focus and the Bullet Journal are prime examples of the no mess no fuss application of the good old pen-to-paper rhythm. Easy, personable, and adaptable, I couldn't recommend the analogue methods enough.

Recap.

A life hack is a way of doing things that is more time-efficient, and therefore better. In other words, it is a strategy, technique, or tool.

As it relates to Thinkers and Doers, an agile result is a complete framework of how to deal with your tasks and goals, both short and long term. The acronym TEA stands for time, energy, and attention. The idea is that you cannot manage time by itself; you must be aware of how you spend your energy and what has your attention. Building an association with it that will prompt you to work.

GTD simply stands for getting things done. You should not keep anything in your head. Instead, you ought to capture it and organize it in the most appropriate list.

The rapid planning method (RPM) focuses on outcomes. RPM encourages us to look at our results; our purpose for going after them, and the actions needed to get us closer. This helps us to avoid taking random steps towards unclear outcomes, which is an unproductive use of our TEA.

Kanban involves using physical space to create three columns: To-Do, Doing, and Done. You then add post-it notes with tasks written on them and place them in the relevant columns. This ensures a smooth workflow and avoids you becoming over-encumbered.

Using spreadsheets can be helpful for larger tasks. You can collect all your action-steps, add a column for tracking different stages and get a lot of utility out of Google sheets or any other spreadsheet app out there.

Take the things you wish to achieve in a year and plan it over 12 weeks. This may improve your chances of getting on and actually executing your goals.

Questions for Reflection:

- Which of these methods do you see being helpful to you?

- Does visualization help you?

- What might be holding you back?

Applications

Being familiar with the digital tools available is important, we are living in a predominantly digitized world. There are many tools available, but I have narrowed it down to the most effective, efficient ones – according to research, personal use, and feedback.

I hope to share this so that you may gain a bit of a head start on the market, sifting through the noise of the life hacker community and getting down to doing. The other reason for sharing this is to caution you; there is no perfect method to managing your lives, there is only the method that is right for you. Don't settle for one method over another for the sake of it being free, or popular, settle on the one that works best.

Trello

Trello is a web-based application that is similar to a Kanban board; in fact, it essentially is a virtual Kanban. With it, you create cards for certain columns. It is a beautifully simple application that is largely compatible with other software, it even has a social feature that allows you to collaborate and share with other members. Plus, it's free.

Trello is one of the most popular of its kind. It's designed well and there are a lot of reviews and how-to guides for it online. It is especially useful for visual Thinkers and Doers. I use it for managing tasks; I use it to organize the Thinker Vs Doer podcast, a project I share in-app with my Co-Host; I use it to maintain an accountability board with a good friend living in New York; I even use it for menial things like groceries.

Asana

Another application though not explicitly intended for implementing a GTD style of list management, nor a Kanban style. It does however provide you with the option of using either or both. If you want lists, boards, and calendars all in one app, Asana is a good choice.

Freedcamp

Not to be confused with the Basecamp app. Both are organizational tools, Freedcamp was released sometime after the more popular Basecamp. Freedcamp implements the same style of project management, it allows you to manage everything from people and teams, to notes and projects.

Chances are you will hear about Basecamp first. One of the best things about this app is that it allows you to figure how it can work best for you, it's versatile. These are both apps that are most useful for project management, so small businesses or start-ups will gain the most out of them.

OmniFocus

This is another GTD style application, only this one is exclusive to Apple products. OmniFocus is one of the two front-runners of the GTD styled task management systems - the other, is Things. I've used both, along with some of the others I have already mentioned. Although I would recommend either as perfectly sound methods of task management, they aren't free. When you compare them to some other free apps available, you may cop for the freebie. However, there are certainly good reasons for the cost, and I do believe you will get your money's worth.

OmniFocus has a weekly review feature, so that you remember to check-in with your projects. It is also a useful tool if you generally work within the Apple ecosystem, syncing your device with your desktop or iPad is useful.

Things

Things is a list management system designed to implement the GTD approach, allowing you to break your goals into three categories: areas, projects, and tasks. You get a fairly minimal interface with which you can plan everything you need to do. There is the option to create groupings of lists and tags, which I like to refer to as the secret fourth category: context.

I've used Things for several years now. I use it to manage everything from personal projects, work projects, business, to household tasks. Work takes up about a third of my day, the rest of my life needs organizing, too! Things makes separating my work and personal life straightforward, I dare say easy.

Questions for Reflection:

- What areas of your life could benefit from the use of digital tools to get you more productive?

- Which tool seems like a logical entry point for you to start exploring the available options out there?

Self-Testing for Doers

Come up with a list of 5-10 ideas that strike you as good and important, then enter them onto your personal calendar with a two-week deadline. After two weeks, you essentially have a meeting with yourself to see how many of those ideas you actually made progress on and completed.

People tend to not answer the question of how they're doing thoughtfully or specifically, but if you have checkpoints and measurements you can begin to understand how you're getting on. Testing yourself to see if you are a Doer, and how you do things is a valuable understanding. Testing for this and reviewing your results will allow you know where you're at, where you've come from, and how fast you can get to where you want to be.

Knowing your pace is powerful, because you can then plan realistically and set yourself the right challenges.

A Valuable Benchmark

We need a way to identify our starting point in order to make progress. In effect, we will need to find out how productive we are now, so that we know how productive we need to become. Identifying this will also give you an indication to whether you are more of a Thinker or a Doer.

The principle is similar to a physical fitness test, in that by taking the test, you must do the physical exercise. You will be applying the action right off the bat. This benchmark is valuable because you will gain a better overview of how to proceed and achieve your desired results.

Once we have tested for our starting position and discovered where we are on the productivity scale, we can measure short-term progress as well as long-term. This is important for self-confidence, and motivation. You will be able to see how you improved from one month to the next, even day to day. This helps us to appreciate specific self-evident truths about our skills and capabilities.

This is why we need benchmarks; to be able to see how we are doing and improving through action. Without a benchmark, your perception of your progress and goals will remain like the horizon, always in the distance.

Self-Confidence

Despite our tendency to prefer comfort and routine over change, human beings are highly adaptable and thrive in challenge. When you begin your journey to a more productive lifestyle, the actions you found difficult soon become your new normal, paving way for new challenges to keep you growing and becoming more of the person you desire to be.

Going from Thinker to Doer is a process that takes time to integrate into routine. As you take on the challenges you face, your confidence grows, and you shed those crippling feelings of self-doubt and fear. This new and more able-minded perception is an important influence on your reality; your success is a reflection of what you believe you are capable of. You have to be able to see yourself moving forward and winning, in order to become that person and not simply dream of becoming.

Having proof of progress will build confidence, and it allows you to gain more control over your self-image.

Journaling

Keep a journal of consistent entries - I suggest either daily or weekly. Your entries ought to be connected to your ideas, obligations, and goals. This works like a less daunting to-do list. Write down your plans, present and future. This serves as a way to consolidate your emotions and your state of mind with your goals and desires.

Review the things you planned to do last week and discover how consistent you are with yourself. If there is a subject you're interested in exploring, get it down in plan form. This doesn't mean you must see it through - perhaps it's a fleeting fancy – but it gets you into the habit of thinking productively. E.g. if you were going to become a fitness instructor, how might you go about it?

The other gain is figuring the lag between when you say you're going to do something and the time it takes you to actually get it done. You may even notice issues you weren't aware of, perhaps there is a pattern between the number of things you plan and the amount you actually do. Are you giving yourself too much at one time?

You can use a calendar in the same way. The gap between Thinkers and Doers is usually based on the individual's level of commitment, using either of these test methods will show you yours.

Questions for Reflection:

- Are you a thinker or a doer? Which resonates more?

- How can you get an accurate baseline of your tendencies and your pace so that you can plan for how you work?

- As you go through your journey, what are some ways that you can use to document your progress besides journaling?

How to Do

Most people need to learn how to do, even if their natural inclination is Doer. The biggest misconception surrounding the concept of doing is that by engaging in or completing a task, we have been productive; we believe by performing an action we have achieved something of value. In fact, the dissonance we experience in working and remaining unsatisfied lies in our habits; procrastination is technically an action, but it is one that is aimed at the wrong thing.

When we feel that we must move from Thinker to Doer, we assume this means we must simply do more. That is exactly the type of misunderstanding that gives room for hiding places. These hiding places are the reason we feel stuck and unsatisfied. We may be taking actions, but these are directed toward things that are not bringing us closer to what we actually desire.

Instead of harboring this type of misconception, we must remove all possible hiding places within us and decide what truly matters. The shift then, is not motivated by becoming a Doer, it is motivated by the results we want. The Doer is the middleman – a means to an end. The common mistake we make is putting the means above the end; the doing before the result. We believe it is the action alone that matters, but it is the result to which the action can take you that matters. If we deem a result worthy of effort, we are on the right track.

Let's Get Physical

Literally, our body, the shape we are in, and the amount of energy we capacitate has an effect on how we do things. A wonderfully accurate and crude example is trying to concentrate with a full bladder. This isn't a fun experience, and eventually you cannot go on. Our physicality influences our Thinker and our Doer. Our diets and activities effect how our brains function – this is a fact, whether your bacon and eggs every morning likes it or not.

Human beings may be intelligent, emotional, even spiritual creatures, but your brain and body are machines. We need nutritional food, hydration, and sleep in order to function effectively; we have to make sure we give the machine the fuel to think and do.

Emotion

Our emotional state is as important as our physical. The way you feel about time, activities, yourself, your life, it all comes into play when it's time to get doing.

The way we feel shapes our perceptions, experiences, and our memories. I maintain that time is something felt, therefore what you feel will affect your ability to apply yourself to an action, and how you think about said action. There are two ways to look at an uncomfortable situation, you can either say, "There's no point in being here.", or "I'm just glad to be here.". Taking care of our emotional wellbeing is a priority. We ought to check-in with ourselves daily. We have to be able to understand where we are emotionally, and learn what we need to feel stable, secure, able, and confident.

Doing Mistakes

I have found that people tend to dig shallow when it comes to reasoning their actions. It is much easier to do without thinking; applying self-control will sometimes seem unfavorable. It's challenging to dig deep and inspect the roots of what it is we desire, often because we trick ourselves by believing that will ruin everything.

Besides, thinking deeply or analytically isn't exactly the standard. If you haven't been connected with productive people you won't recognize this type of thinking as normal. Unfortunately, what is taught is superficial and so that is what many of us become used to. An example of this is the general reaction to a study done in the 1950s on traits associated with a higher risk of heart disease: The type-A personalities were stress-prone individuals who did not take time to relax and recoup; The public admired the type-A personality based on the loose notion of them being go-getters and high-achievers. Despite the context of the study people encouraged this personality type, ignoring its indication to an early grave.

When we follow this notion of looking busy rather than being productive, we don't recognize it as a mistake. Activity isn't necessarily progress. Avoiding actions that require change and self-discipline isn't freedom. These mistakes are what keeps us from the results we want.

I had a coach named Kerrul Kassel. She had some videos on productivity. One in particular changed my perception of options: she spoke on the differences between tasks, goals, and objectives in relation to action and purpose. If you're focused on going to the gym, there are several things you could be after. Usually we will take an activity and set a goal around it, without considering the reason we might want it. Do you believe losing weight will make you feel better about your health, or is it about your self-image? In this hypothetical, we're figuring out your objective, through which we can decide if the joining a gym is the best action to take.

Instead of jumping into a task with a vague idea of how it might help you, consider your objectives. Dig deeper.

Questions for Reflection:

- Are there any actions that you're currently taking that may be aimed at the wrong results and how can you correct those?

- What are the results that you are after and what could you do to audit those actions to ensure they are aligned with your goals?

- Are there any doing mistakes that you're making that could be keeping you from your objectives?

Versus

The title of this book is ironic really, as there is in fact no intended competition between the Thinker and the Doer. It is a balance of the two that we are after. For some, one will weigh heavier than the other, and in order to maintain a balance you must first recognize who the predominant winner is within you. We have to know which player to substitute in or out and when, according to the task.

The aim of thinking is to ask the right questions and get the proper definitions in place. It is to clarify what needs to be done and focus on the reasons you do it. Doing, on the other hand, is taking the right actions. It is making sure that actions matter for your purpose. The Thinker and the Doer must dance the dance of balance. If the Thinker always takes the lead, the Doer will be passive; nothing will be done – vice versa.

Balance will allow for the most efficient, purposeful, and powerful execution of any given goal. You have to play them off of each other.

The False Narrative of Thinking vs Doing

Counter intuitively, these two modes of being are not opposed to one another. They work hand-in-hand. The amount of time you might spend ineffectively thinking about what you are going to do, reduces the amount of quality work done. If you believe being a Thinker is the lesser, and you aim to stop being a Thinker, all you will achieve is a new a hiding place.

The fact of the matter is, there are many places to hide from work, the biggest of these is the trap of believing that you either don't think enough and do without thinking, or you don't do enough and you overthink.

Hiding Doers

The Doer that does not think will hide in the belief that their actions don't pay off and dismiss it by saying they were never thinking about it anyway. This is a lack of taking responsibility for one's actions, and perhaps more importantly, one's results. This will then prevent them from coming up with better solutions or learning from their mistakes – the biggest of which, would be the fact that they did not think things through.

Hiding Thinkers

The Thinker hides within a state of perpetual inaction. They will blame their inaction on overthinking, and not on the simple fact that they did not take action. Thinkers need to learn to direct their thoughts, and apply actions to their thinking, only then can they move forward.

Deploying Your Thinkers and Doers

Ultimately, you want to be able to understand when best to deploy one mode over the other; when they must work together, and when one ought to take the lead in a given moment. Learning to deploy team Think and team Do appropriately is how you will achieve the results you desire.

It is all about your objective. The Thinker will help you to get clear on your objective, the Doer will help identify which action provides the best result. The goal then isn't to do as much as possible, it is to get as many results as possible.

You want to make sure that you are setting your modes up for success, by applying them to what they do best. It's not a matter of putting the Thinker against the Doer, it is putting them both to work so that you get the results you want.

Questions for Reflection:

- Which objectives that you're after could do better if you spent more time thinking about it?

- And what about those objectives that need more action? What steps could you take today to move them forward?

- Are there any challenges that would benefit from a combined deployment of the thinker and the doer to get the job done?

Do it Like a Thinker

How to take action and produce outcomes using lessons from coders and engineers – the Thinkers of our time.

There are many Thinkers across the eras that have been known for their results. There are likely to be other great Thinkers whom no one has ever heard of. What might have been the difference? When we think of Da Vinci, Edison, Emerson, we associate great thinking and invention to them. This is because these men were balanced Thinkers and Doers, and they possessed a spirit of experimentation.

If you sit alone and come up with solutions to difficult problems, but you do no work toward those solutions, your mind has gone to waste and no one will benefit.

Show and Tell

One of my favorite scenes in The Grinch is Grinch thinking up ways to avoid going into town by the invite of Cindy Lou Who. He reviews his agenda for the day and one of his to-dos stood out: "Solve world hunger. Tell no one." For me, this scene is funny every time because it resonates with me. It is true of Thinkers to find solutions for problems, solutions that will never see the light of day because the Thinkers refuse to show their work and tell anyone.

I am a Thinker first; I ponder, I dream, I plan, I conjure wonderful images of a better future. Thinkers know how to come up with better ways to do things. The one thing that separates the Thinkers we admire and the ones we've never heard of, is the former showed their work.

If you hide your thoughts away, no-one will ever know of them and you will never know if your solutions actually work. Until you bring an idea into reality, you will not know its value.

How and Where to Show and Tell

You can speak, write, publish, or license your work. Some research ought to be done before choosing a where. Finding the best place to share depends on the type of work you have to show. Usually, there aren't such strict rules, so long as it is accessible for public view and/or use.

Being notable used to be far more difficult, there used to be much more work involved in arranging a space for the public to access you and your work. Now we have the internet and social medias. Of course, this isn't always positive as it means absolutely anyone with access to the internet can share their thoughts and opinions, while that is the essence of freedom of speech, it isn't always that the people are coherent or intelligible. Nonetheless, the internet is a brilliant platform.

Personally, I hated the concept of self-promotion. Now I understand its necessity and usefulness, I have a podcast, Instagram, and Facebook, all of which I use to share my ideas and promote my work. If you have ideas worth sharing - ideas that bring value to the lives of others - you have a responsibility to share it. Recognizing a worthy idea is simple, what does it offer other people? It is an exchange, a trade; for the public's time and attention, you provide them with some valuable idea or service. If you have no such thing to present, why share at all?

You ought to be able to communicate in a way that will allow others to receive it.

Tweet it, 'gram it, post it on Facebook; put it in a book or upload a video. In one way or another, put your work in a form more tangible than thought.

How Thinkers Do

Make assertions about what you're thinking. Then capture those thoughts and stand behind your beliefs.

Like scientists, we have to hypothesize and theorize first in order to test something and discover whether it works or is true. Don't hide behind the veil of luck, capture your beliefs and put them to test. If you believe something to be true, or you believe you can do something, stand by that proclamation and prove it. Following and even during this, show your work. What were your experiments? What did you find? How did you deal with struggles?

This is how Thinkers do. They clarify, test, then execute. All the while documenting the process, sharing their findings. The world will only know what you allow it to understand; it can only benefit from you through interaction. Don't be a Grinch! If you can solve world-hunger, tell everyone.

Questions for Reflection:

- Do you have any projects that could benefit from less doing and showing and telling?

- Are you hoarding any solutions that could be helpful to others if you take the steps to share them?

- What platforms and medium would you consider using to start showing and sharing your work more consistently?

Part III

Real Problems vs First-World Problems

When I succumb to inaction, whether that inaction is toward something trivial or something important, it is always due to either procrastination, or a lack of follow-through.

What is interesting about this fact is that when it comes to real problems, I know what to do – we all do. It is as if we are trained for the life-death scenarios; we have instincts. If I am starving, I eat. If I am in danger, I know that I need to fight or flee. However, when the problem we face is more of a first-world issue - the seemingly softer needs like self-actualization - we have a much harder time doing what needs to be done. The issue then is that we confuse basic needs and practicality with first-world problems, and we don't know how to move on out of this. This is where trained thinking helps.

Which is Which

When you're faced with a dilemma, the first thing you ought to do is deploy your Thinker. You must ask yourself questions and probe the issue, in other words, perform a risk assessment.

The questions are always the same; it's the subject matter that changes. Questions will help you identify whether you are dealing with a real problem, or an imaginary one. Once you know which it is, you are able to take an action.

We tend to spend too much time putting off thinking something over, time that could be used to solve the problems at hand. There are the usual questions we ask, relating to pain or pleasure, but there are others too.

The Five-Fold Why is a tool interpreted by Josh Kaufman in The Personal MBA. This technique requires you to ask yourself why you want something and continue asking why until you're five levels deep in trying to understand, getting closer to the truest reason. By spending this time getting to know all the things you want, you can prioritize them accordingly, making it easier to make the right decisions and doing so efficiently. After all, you don't want to be too busy self-actualizing when you should be putting food on the table.

When we handle issues in the best-prioritized order, it naturally becomes easier to maintain clarity and do the things we want to make happen. We do not necessarily need motivation to satisfy certain physical desires, it is only when we oppose something for some reason that we require motivation.

How to Clarify

Considering Maslow's hierarchy of needs, if the problem you're dealing with is going to work its way down the hierarchy, then it's a real problem. This is how to distinguish one from the other.

Some people will decide against doing something because of first-world issues, like not joining the gym because people will look at them and think they look weird running, or something to that effect. This is an example of putting problems in the wrong order. The Maslow hierarchy of needs is physical before social; if you were stranded in the desert, literally starving to death and dangerously dehydrated, and you managed to find your way to a small roadside diner, only to go in and find that the bread isn't gluten-free and they only serve tap water, will you turn and walk out? You wouldn't! You will eat that glutenous bread and chug that tap water because your life depends on it.

Take the time to sift through the problems prevalent in your life and put them in their proper place. This hierarchy notion is a brilliant tool for clarifying and prioritizing needs.

Questions for Reflection:

- Are there projects, goals, and objectives on your list that need to be re-examined through the lens of a real world vs. first-world viewpoint?

The Four Stages of Competence

This is a matter of psychology: the concept of there being four levels of competence; unconscious incompetence, conscious incompetence; conscious competence, and unconscious competence.

The first of these is a state of ignorance - you don't know that you don't know. The second is knowing that you don't know something, a state we will find ourselves in if we are actively learning something.

The last two are the competent levels. If we are consciously competent, we know what we are doing but we have to think in order to do it. This stage is similar to having a driving permit, in that you know how to drive well-enough to have passed your test, but you still require learning practice. The final level is unconscious competence, the functioning of our organs falls into this category. This level of competence can lend itself to other activities, too. Unconscious competence is being able to perform an action without thinking. The idea that you will never forget how to ride a bike is true, because you've built the necessary neural pathway for that action, and you have ridden your bike so consistently that you've strengthened that pathway. It becomes a simple matter of taking the action, the rest is natural. The principle is the same in practicing a thinking or doing method, you eventually become unconsciously competent at it – this is what a habit is.

Unconscious Competence

Achieving unconscious competence means understanding and developing your idea of how you learn. There is so much to internalize and practice, the best way to make sure you do not become overwhelmed by the information, the methods, the tactics, and the practices, is to break it down into chunks.

The fastest, most effective way to do this is researching how people learn new things, specifically in situations where there is a lot to digest. From there, we snowball out learning.

The 4-Step Productivity Snowball

First, we find the simplest, most straightforward productivity booster and stick to it. Set yourself between one to three goals and write down one action per goal that you need to take to move closer to that goal. Aim to achieve this by the following day.

Secondly comes the hump. This is the obstacle you have to get over. By now you will have used this simple booster technique for at least four weeks. The idea is that you don't overload yourself with too many new things to learn and do. Instead, you focus on the practice of getting better at showing up to that appointment with yourself and become comfortable with following through. You will begin to trust in your ability to see your own commitments through. By the time you gain this new confidence in yourself, you will ideally have gone from unconscious incompetence to conscious competence. What is important to realize here is that you have added onto your toolbelt – something you did not have before. You now have a trusted method to apply self-discipline.

The third step is to now use this newly internalized productivity routine to level-up your system. Start setting new goals, plan your next learning curve, try a new method or concept you would like to explore or understand better. The rule is to maintain your existing system. Learning a new method doesn't mean throwing out the first one, it means building on the top of it.

The fourth step is to stop, every so often taking stock and reviewing what has worked and what hasn't. Think of it as trimming the fat for the health of the system. Be sure not to obsess over this process, it isn't to be practiced every day.

Autopilot

I've said it before and I'll say it again, practice truly does make the master. When we practice an action or thought process enough, we eventually can switch to autopilot.

There are things I can do that, having practiced, require very little thought. If I need to express something in writing I can get the words out of my head and onto the page effortlessly. I can even lay down bars for a freestyle battle on a whim, not the most relevant skill I have, but it's still a skill I have. There are also many things I know I cannot do fluently, or at all, because I have not had the practice.

When you imagine being able to run on autopilot, able to simply show up and do the thing you're so good at, you ought to be careful of getting carried away on that confidence wave. There are no permanent habits. Habits, by nature, can and will change depending on the attention you give them; the more resistance there is to hold onto an idea, the harder it is to change it – vice versa.

If you achieve unconscious competence, you must make sure that you keep up the practice, because something can always distract or lure you away from it. Rather than believing you can run on autopilot, it is of better value for you to view this confidence and ability as a system – or habit – you have set that works for you. Commit to it in this way and stay vigilant in pursuing its continuation and growth in your life. After all, this is the greatest execution tool; showing up and just doing.

Questions for Reflection:

- What skills do you have that you can recall going through the four stages of competence?

- What lessons from other areas of skill and habit acquisition can you apply to your growth in the area of clear thinking and productive doing?

Thinking About Doing Something

Thinking about doing [blank] is the head-space you want to be in when it comes to improving your quality of life, whether it's personal or career oriented. Thinking about thinking will only do so much for you; thinking about doing is where the real progress lies. When action follows thought, you know you are on your way.

Your thoughts should be the starting point for your progress on the idea, and the issues preventing you from turning idle thoughts into vision, and vision into reality. If your thoughts make your problems clearer and help you discover a solution, you are merely dwelling on a problem. It will do you no good to solely focus on the definition and clarification part of thought, action must follow.

Action is a deliverance of sorts. This is why I advocate setting your thoughts onto paper; the physicality of words on paper represents thought quite clearly, and therefore allows for a clearer perspective of where you're at. Words on a page, that is, to-do styled lists, won't be what moves you toward your goal, it is the promise and execution of the associated actions.

How Will I Know When to Stop Thinking?

In trying to solve a problem, you will initially spend time getting clarified: What is the issue I'm trying to solve?", "What is preventing me from solving it?", and "What do I want the outcome to be?". Once you have these answers, you can then shift focus to solutions. You should spend as much time as is necessary for you to figure out what you want, why you want it, how you will know when it succeeds, and what your next step will be. It is largely a natural process, you will know when you're finished if you begin with these identifiers.

If you are not producing something tangible, some kind of evidential proof of progress, then it becomes too easy for you to deceive yourself by concluding your hard work hasn't paid off. You should be able to show and tell. By sharing your progress and results with others, or documenting it for your personal review, you are confirming your improvements.

Think of this as solving potential problems for your future-self. Use your time to its fullest extent and let go of the expectation of being at a constant state of optimal performance – let go of perfectionism.

How Can I Use Over-Thinking to My Advantage?

This can be tricky, it is easy to slip up here. Using your natural tendency to over-think to your advantage means learning how to contain your thinking habits, and separate thinking as its own task.

There are many types of thinking, over-thinkers predominantly worry and daydream by default. It is important to start breaking down your thoughts. There are several ways to do so and, depending on the situation, you will need to set aside time to make those happen.

We all think, but not all of us know how to think in a way that works for us. Instead, we perceive thinking as an independent entity within our minds. The truth is, it is a matter of getting behind the wheel and learning to take control. We ought to treat our brains with the respect it deserves – in order to get the best use of it.

Directed Thinking

Pick a question, topic, or problem and allow your mind to explore it. This is directed thinking, and the only recommendable form of productive thought. This is the initiation to all other types of thought. Guide your mind through what you want it to work on, rather than being passive.

Clarified Thinking

Clarified thinking comes once you understand what you want. This type of thinking is second to directed thinking. It lets you know what you want, so that you can go and get it and know when you've got it - and to recognize when you've missed it.

Having goals, setting outcomes, and having vision are all parts of clarified thinking.

Next-Level Thinking

Next-level thinking is essentially having vision. Vision is a big part of progress for both practice, and method. Figuring out your next move is how you get your project on a trajectory and maintain momentum.

Vision is highly underrated, yet so important. You don't have to know every step you're going to make, only the very next one. This is the best way to keep on keeping on. Having a consistent thought-ladder of doing one more thing, taking one more step then taking the step after that, and so on. Repetition then is what is needed to reach your predetermined outcome. That is the game; the Thinker discovers the next step as the Doer completes the previous step.

Visionary Thinking

Vision is allowing yourself to see ultimate possibilities and believing you can arrive at the ends of those possibilities. Thinking as a visionary is to see your place in the future you desire. Despite its simple explanation, it is a difficult thought process to maintain.

The difficulty is in looking beyond current or potential circumstance and instead, seeing yourself lead the life you want to live. Having this clarity gives you an understanding of the effects of your daily decisions, so that you may live in a way that will allow you to confidently step into your future.

It is a matter of imagination and projectile thinking. The effect of visionary thinking on motivation is the same as experiencing a tangible outcome of work, like receiving a paycheck at the end of the month. Vision is the passion and motivation we all need in order to direct our lives and succeed.

Purposeful Thinking

Purposeful thinking are thoughts grounded in reasons, reasons that compel actions. It cannot be said enough, that spending the time to understand your *whys* is something that will propel you through the stages of action and thought.

Solution Oriented Thinking

This is the type of thinking that requires a degree of hopefulness or faith. The decision to look in the direction of a solution, as opposed to the idle dwelling on problems and consequence.

Your mission will have obstacles, this is an inevitability, so be clear with yourself on this from the beginning. When these occur, we release the Thinker and dissect the problems to come to conclusive reviews of them. We do this in order to move passed them and progress further; to be better equipped in our pursuit of our goals.

Questions for Reflection:

- What are some actions on your plate that need more clarification?

- Is there a project that could benefit from more visionary thinking?

- Are there areas where your motivation is fading that could use more purposeful thinking to reignite your intensity for completion?

The Five Terms of Action

Understanding the definitions of these five terms within the context of the productive space will help you to communicate your dreams to yourself, and to others.

For successful communication to take place, people must be honest in their pursuits of understanding and knowledge and be on the same page in relation to the use of specific language. Otherwise, we will find ourselves in a room full of dreamers throwing around words and concepts they do not understand to the point where all meaning is lost, only to disperse back into your own lives none-the-wiser.

You ought to understand these terms by their proper definitions, to evoke your intended meaning by them.

Project

A project is the intentional undertaking of predetermined steps for the purpose of achieving a specific outcome.

A project isn't an idea, it is the plan that follows an idea. The necessary steps toward the specified outcome ought to have been considered, implemented, and planned for. When you call something a project, be sure that you are referring to something substantial; explainable with details and definitions.

Outcome

Outcome is a loaded word. People tend to resist defining their intention for a project either due to a lack of clarification or a worry-soaked refusal to show and tell. The word ensues focus, specificity, and confidence in what you want.

Defining your outcome can also help you in planning your project. You can use the end as a means to itself by working your way backward and finding out what actions need taking.

Objective

Objective is the subtitle to Goal. In its simplest definition, an objective is what you seek to come from your goal. The less trivial pursuits in life will usually require a step or two further into the *why*; we aim for one thing, and with the gain of that thing comes spoils – or sub-goals.

Aiming to earn $1,000 is a goal, the objective then is what you hope to gain from that amount of money. I have found that our objectives are usually based in emotion, rather than the more logical, lateral part of our minds. Understanding these emotion-based objectives will help you to operate more freely for the sake of your projects.

Result

This is the simplest of them all. A result is the consequence of an action. It is more of a developmental tool than a conclusion.

Goal

The bull's-eye the archer shoots for. Goals are specific, realistic, and time-bound. It should also be a form of proof or confirmation, and a sign as to whether or not you have reached your objective(s).

Questions for Reflection:

- Think of an area in your life that you feel that nagging feeling to change it, and ask yourself – what are you after? What is your goal?

- What would the outcome look like if you successfully achieved this goal?

- Could you break down this goal in projects that if completed would lead to the results your after?

- What would those projects look like?

My Project

My aim was to lend you the tools you need to lift yourself up and out of the survival slump, and into the joyousness of living purposefully. I wanted to encourage you to keep learning and building, to live your calling and lead a good life.

Further, I hope to have reached the men and women with real responsibilities: family, financial stability. Those who have been too tired and too drained for too long and have so far lacked the proper me-time they deserve. For me to call this book a success, it would take the knowledge that from what I have shared, people have begotten the hope of a better future. I want readers to understand that there are ways they can organize projects and achieve goals. This book is a motivation and a guide for you to succeed.

Completing this project means I earn the title of Author; becoming the person I want to be, a person who actually does the thing they say they want to do. I have been talking about writing a book for the last 10 years, I will finally be living up to my potential and helping people bring their own objectives to reality. This completion can be tied to my identity for the rest of my life, and I can take pride and be glad in the results of my hard work – the words I have written were time boxed and delivered, perhaps not refined, but nonetheless, done (Apologies to my Editor!).

Someday someone is going to tell me that they read my book, and if I'm able to help just one person kick-start their life when they thought it was too late for them, if all of these things are felt and realized, my objectives will have been met.

If I had decided to give up on this project, I would have lost a little respect for myself and my confidence in my ability to do what I say would have taken a blow, but I saw it through, and I now know at a deeper level that when I set my mind to something, I can do it. I like who that makes me and what that makes me feel.

This project is not about me and it never was, it was about a friend that I was trying to help get out of his head and take some action. But by following through on my plans, I can now say that I am a go-getter, a hard-worker; I am someone that wins. It is not about how others view my success nor me; it is about me and the things that I can say I am. I do not quit when things become difficult; I double down and follow through. That leads us to define: who are you?

Survival vs Living

Go and get clear on what you want and why you want it. What does success look like to you, and how do you see yourself in that success? Figure out the steps you need to take to make it all happen and do the work. And when you run out of work, find new goals, new steps, new success to aim for. When you lose your motivation, remind yourself of your *whys* and revisit that vision of success. Then, get back to work.

Don't give up, adapt and stay grounded. Ask for help when you need it; be accountable. Most importantly, decide what winning means for you, and start living it. Dream bigger and work smarter. If you're ready to go from idea to done, help yourself to my free *Project Starter E-Course* by visiting http://thinkervsdoer.com/bonuses for more details.

About the Author

John-Paul Adams lives in Dallas TX, by way of NYC and CT. Born in Nigeria, he loves productivity, efficiency, systems thinking and coding.

His interest in personal growth, meta-learning, and success, started more than 20 years ago and has never waned. By day he works as an IT Leader at a Global Oil & Gas company. And when he doesn't have his hands full with his family, he's trying to figure out ways to help more thinkers to execute and get more results on their goals.

One Last Thing

If you enjoyed this book or found it useful, I would be grateful if you would post a short review on Amazon. Your support really does make a difference and I read all the reviews personally.

Thanks again for your support!

If you would like to get in touch, please do contact me via **Instagram** or **Facebook** @jpadamsonline.